# China-India Relations: Tensions Persist Despite Growing Cooperation

# Executive Summary

Despite growing bilateral cooperation between China and India, sources of tension in the relationship remain and in some cases are becoming more pronounced. In the security realm, continued occurrences of Chinese soldiers crossing into disputed areas of the China-India border and China's growing presence in the Indian Ocean are sources of friction in China-India relations. In the economic realm, India has a large trade imbalance with China, due to the distortionary effects of China's economic policy, Chinese competitiveness in export-oriented industries, and India's economic and institutional problems.

Meanwhile, the 2012-2013 leadership transition in China and the 2014 election of Prime Minister Narendra Modi in India have increased potential for bilateral cooperation. The two countries seek to work together on a growing number of issues, including stability in Afghanistan and climate change. In addition, during Chinese President Xi Jinping's visit to India in September 2014, China pledged to invest in Indian industrial parks and high-speed rail infrastructure. China and India also are collaborating in multilateral forums and institutions, such as the summits of Brazil, Russia, India, China, and South Africa (BRICS) and the new BRICS development bank.

Although both governments seek to reduce tension in the relationship, the potential for competition, miscalculation, and conflict between the two countries persists. For the United States, Prime Minister Modi's election and India's evolving strategic calculations have important implications for U.S. security interests, and may present opportunities for greater U.S.-India military and security cooperation. The United States also could cooperate with India to promote a greater balance of economic power in the Asia Pacific region, encourage improved market access in China, promote Chinese compliance with its World Trade Organization (WTO) obligations, and enhance global energy security.

# Overview of the China-India Relationship

Although China and India have been strategic rivals since the mid-twentieth century, in recent years China has become India's largest trading partner and the Indian government is now more supportive of Chinese investment, which is limited but growing.[1] Like many other Asian states, India faces the challenge of balancing its desire to expand economic ties with China with its apprehension about China's strategic intentions, particularly along the disputed China-India border and in the Indian Ocean.

The two countries' leaders have sought to reduce bilateral tensions.[2] The 2012-2013 leadership transition in China and the 2014 election of Prime Minister Modi in India present new opportunities for cooperation.[3] However, despite cooperative initiatives and official statements emphasizing positive areas of the relationship,[4] Asia's two largest rising powers, both of whom possess nuclear weapons, distrust each other, and each is sensitive to the other operating in its respective area of influence.[5] In the security realm, major sources of tension in the relationship are the China-India border dispute, China's activities in the Indian Ocean, China-Pakistan relations, and Tibet. In the economic realm, India faces an increasingly unbalanced trade relationship with China, and the two countries are competing for access to energy supplies.

# Areas of Tension

## China-India Border Dispute

The chief irritant between China and India is their disputed border in the Himalayas, where a Line of Actual Control (LAC)[*] demarcates an effective boundary. The LAC runs along the southern part of the Aksai Chin region, the northern part of Sikkim State, and the northern part of Arunachal Pradesh State (see Figure 1).

**Figure 1: Disputed China-India Border Areas**

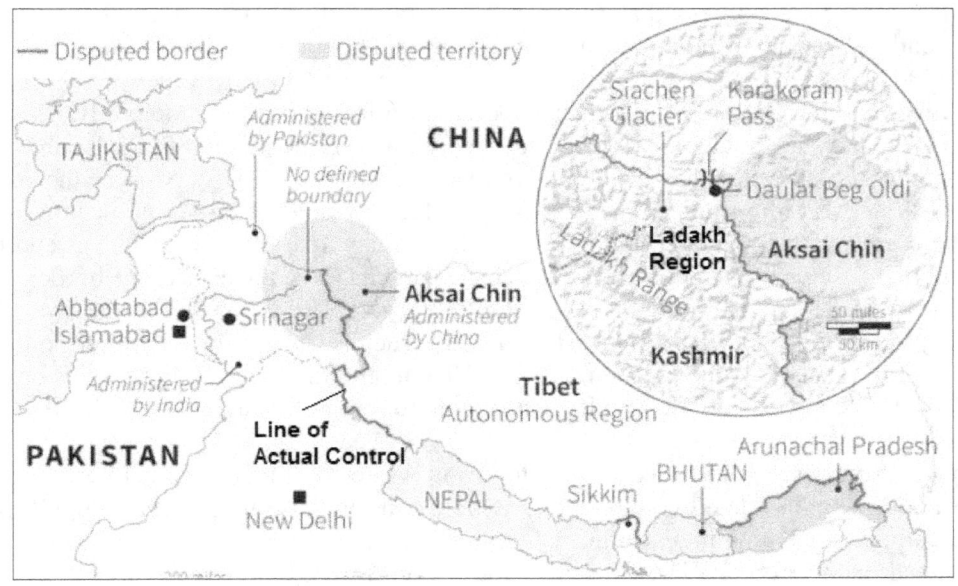

*Source:* Alyssa Ayers, "China's Mixed Messages to India," *Asia Unbound* (Council on Foreign Relations Blog), September 17, 2014. *http://blogs.cfr.org/asia/2014/09/17/chinas-mixed-messages-to-india/.* Adapted by the authors.

China and India engaged in a war and several smaller confrontations between 1962 and the mid-to-late 1980s. India suffered a humiliating defeat in 1962 when China launched a month-long attack into Arunachal Pradesh and the Ladakh region. The two countries had several small military confrontations along their shared border over the next 25 years and in 1986-1987 came close to another war.[6]

---

[*] China and India informally delineated the LAC following the ceasefire that ended the Sino-Indian war of 1962. The two countries officially accepted the LAC in a bilateral agreement in 1993. The LAC, however, is ill-defined, in part due to the complex topography of the Ladakh region. India and China have different perceptions of the demarcation set by the LAC and have yet to negotiate an official boundary. R. L. Bahtia and Tang Jiaxuan, "Agreement on the Maintenance of Peace along the Line of Actual Control in the India-China Border," (Stimson Center, September 7, 1993). *http://www.stimson.org/research-pages/agreement-on-the-maintenance-of-peace-along-the-line-of-actual-control-in-the-india-china-border/;* Michelle FlorCruz, "Line of Actual Control: China and India Again Squabbling over Disputed Himalayan Border," *International Business Times*, May 3, 2013. *http://www.ibtimes.com/line-actual-control-china-india-again-squabbling-over-disputed-himalayan-border-1236401;* Raja Mohan, *The Sino-Indian Border Dispute and Asian Security* (Strategic and Defense Studies Center, June 2013). *http://ips.cap.anu.edu.au/sites/default/files/COG7.pdf;* and Hongzhou Zhang and Mingjiang Li, "Sino-Indian Border Disputes," *Institute for International Political Studies* 181 (June 2013) 1-9. *http://www.ispionline.it/sites/default/files/pubblicazioni/analysis_181_2013.pdf.*

Beijing and New Delhi agreed to border management protocols in the mid-1990s, and reached additional agreements in 2005 and 2013 that established rules of conduct and confidence building measures between their militaries. Nevertheless, low-level confrontations between border patrols continue to occur. According to New Delhi, China's People's Liberation Army (PLA) soldiers frequently cross disputed portions of the LAC (more than 700 times between January 2013 and August 2014) but do not usually stay there longer than several hours.[7] The Chinese government does not publicize the occurrence of Indian personnel crossing disputed portions of the LAC.

- Most recently, border tensions flared after a contingent of PLA soldiers crossed a disputed portion of the LAC on September 10, 2014 and began building a road, according to Indian media reporting.[8] A standoff between the PLA and the Indian Army ensued, with both sides sending more troops to the border. The crisis ended two weeks later after the Chinese and Indian governments agreed to withdraw troops, a process that ended on September 30.[9] This incident began shortly before President's Xi's visit to India, which raises questions about civil-military coordination in China.

In general, China's military capabilities and transportation infrastructure are more advanced than India's and would give China an advantage in a border conflict. However, the number of PLA combat units in the Tibet Autonomous Region (TAR) has not increased markedly in recent years.[*] Most of the combat units in China's Chengdu and Lanzhou military regions, which likely would be called upon in a major military conflict on the border with India, are based far away in Yunnan and Sichuan provinces and the Xinjiang Uyghur Autonomous Region.[10] In contrast, India is increasing its force levels near the border. This decision likely is driven by India's concern about the gap in military capabilities between the two militaries and China's rapidly developing civilian transportation infrastructure in the TAR, which could be used to transport Chinese troops and equipment to the border. To defend the LAC, Beijing relies on the ability to rapidly reinforce the relatively few PLA units permanently based in the region.

- Through exercises, PLA ground and air forces in western China continue to enhance their ability to respond to India-related contingencies. One recent exercise took place in the TAR in August 2012 and involved a mountain infantry brigade and an air force division conducting an assault on a notional enemy force.[11] The PLA uses these exercises to improve its ability to overcome the challenges of operating in these remote, high-altitude areas.

- China's recent improvements in transportation infrastructure in western China would facilitate PLA troop movements and decrease PLA response time in an Indian contingency. In 2006, Beijing opened a rail line from Qinghai Province to the TAR. China recently extended the rail line farther into the TAR and plans to extend it to the China-India border by 2020. In 2013, China completed a stretch of highway to a county in the TAR near the border; the county was the last in the TAR without a highway connection.[12]

- India is strengthening its military readiness for China-related contingencies by increasing the number of its forward-deployed ground and air forces and holding military exercises in the border region. The Indian Air Force (IAF) plans to deploy two additional squadrons of Su-30 fighter

---

[*] PLA units conducting patrols of China's border with India are border defense units. People's Armed Police (PAP) border security units also conduct patrols of the border. These PLA and PAP units operate from outposts near the border and are usually small and lightly armed. Their primary missions are surveillance and early warning. PLA border defense units are under the command of military sub-district headquarters. PAP border units are under the command of local public security bureaus. Dennis J. Blasko, *The Chinese Army Today: Tradition and Transformation for the 21ˢᵗ Century*, (Oxford, UK: Routledge, 2012), pp. 27, 86; Dennis Blasko, e-mail interview with Commission staff, December 12, 2014; Dennis Blasko, "PLA Ground Force Modernization and Mission Diversification: Underway in All Military Regions," in Roy Kamphausen and Andrew Scobell eds. *Right-sizing the People's Liberation Army: Exploring the Contours of China's Military* (Carlisle, PA, U.S. Army War College, 2007), pp. 300-301.

aircraft to northeastern India.[13] The Indian Army plans to deploy a new mountain strike corps, which will consist of more than 90,000 soldiers and be equipped with mountain artillery and antiaircraft guns, to the LAC.[14] In 2012, the IAF and Indian Army held a military exercise near the China-India border that involved fighter and transport aircraft and special operations personnel.[15]

- India is taking steps to improve its military and transportation infrastructure along the disputed border. In recent years, the IAF reopened airstrips near the LAC to enhance its ability to provide logistical support to Indian personnel on the ground.[16] The Indian government reduced restrictions on construction of roads and military facilities along the LAC and it plans to build 54 new border outposts for the Indo-Tibetan Border Police in Arunachal Pradesh.[17] India also plans to build a 1,118 mile road and three rail lines in Arunachal Pradesh, one of which would be connected to India's Assam State.[18]

## China's Growing Presence in the Indian Ocean

China's military presence in the Indian Ocean has increased considerably over the last five years, almost certainly reflecting China's desire to improve its ability to protect sea routes vital to its economic development. Over 80 percent of China's crude oil imports travel through the Indian Ocean.[19]

- Since January 2009, the PLA Navy has sustained counterpiracy operations in the Gulf of Aden, which is located in the western portion of the Indian Ocean, to protect Chinese commercial shipping interests. The inaugural counterpiracy patrol was China's first operational deployment of naval forces outside China's regional waters, aside from naval diplomacy.[20]

- In 2012, the PLA Navy for the first time began deploying maritime intelligence collection ships to the Indian Ocean.[21] These ships likely have equipment enabling them to collect signals and electronic intelligence and to map the ocean floor,[22] suggesting the PLA Navy may be building the foundation for more routine naval operations in the region in the near term.

- In early 2014, a PLA Navy surface task group conducted a long-distance combat readiness patrol that spanned the South China Sea, eastern Indian Ocean, and Philippine Sea. The deployment marked the first time the PLA Navy conducted a surface combat readiness patrol in the Indian Ocean.[23] Furthermore, from December 2013 to February 2014, a PLA Navy submarine carried out China's first submarine patrol in the Indian Ocean.[24] Although China reportedly told Indian military officials the submarine would be supporting the PLA Navy's ongoing counterpiracy operations in the Gulf of Aden,[25] China also likely used the deployment to test the submarine and its crew's ability to operate for long durations at extended distances from China and to prepare for potential crises and wartime operations in the Indian Ocean. Since then, at least one and potentially two additional PLA Navy submarines have deployed to the Indian Ocean, indicating Chinese submarine patrols in the region are becoming routine.[26]

In recent years, China has played a large role in financing and constructing civilian port infrastructure in the Indian Ocean, including the Ports of Colombo and Hambantota in Sri Lanka,[27] and Gwadar Port in Pakistan.[28] Furthermore, PLA Navy counterpiracy task groups have made port calls in at least 12 regional countries for resupply and replenishment and military-to-military engagements.[29] Chinese investments in commercial ports in the Indian Ocean and Chinese naval diplomacy with countries in the region probably will improve the PLA Navy's ability to replenish supplies and fuel using regional ports, and could lay the groundwork for future logistics hubs in the Indian Ocean.

New Delhi is concerned China's growing military activity and investment in and around the Indian Ocean are designed to encircle India and challenge India's goal of being the primary security guarantor in the Indian Ocean.[30] These are among the factors driving India's ambitious naval modernization program.

- Over the next decade, the Indian Navy plans to expand its power projection capabilities with additional aircraft carriers, major surface combatants, diesel and nuclear-powered submarines, amphibious ships, fighter aircraft, helicopters, and long-range surveillance aircraft (see Table 1 for a full list).[31] In particular, India seeks to strengthen its nuclear deterrent force, and to enhance the Indian Navy's capability to conduct expeditionary operations, secure important sea lanes in the Indian Ocean, and control maritime choke points.[32]

- In 2014, India's major annual naval exercise, TROPEX (Theater Level Operational Readiness Exercise), featured India's new indigenous military surveillance and communications satellite as well as its P-8I maritime patrol aircraft, recently acquired from the United States.[33]

### Table 1: India's Planned Major Air and Naval Acquisitions, 2015-2025

| Platform | Approximate Number |
|---|---|
| Destroyers | 2 KOLKATA-class guided-missile destroyers (being built indigenously)[34] |
| Frigates | 7 stealth frigates (being built indigenously)[35] |
| Diesel Submarines | 6 SCORPENE-class submarines (license acquired from France; being built in India)[36] |
| Nuclear Submarines | 3 ARIHANT-class submarines (being built indigenously);[37] 2 AMUR-class submarines (to be acquired from Russia)[38] |
| Aircraft Carriers | 1 VIKRANT-class carrier (being built indigenously)[39] |
| Amphibious Ships | 4 landing platform docks (contract has not yet been awarded)[40] |
| Maritime Patrol Aircraft | 2 P-8I POSEIDON maritime patrol aircraft (to be acquired from the United States)[41] |
| Helicopters | 16 S-70B SEAHAWK multi-role helicopters (to be acquired from the United States)[42] |
| Fighter Aircraft | 126 RAFALE medium multirole combat aircraft (to be acquired from France)[43] |
| Fighter/Ground Attack Aircraft | 42 Su-30MKI FLANKER fighter aircraft (being jointly developed by India and Russia)[44] |
| Transport Aircraft | 6 C-130J-30 HERCULES transport aircraft (to be acquired from the United States);[45] 5 C-17A GLOBEMASTER transport aircraft (to be acquired from the United States)[46] |

Sources: *Jane's IHS*, *Defense News*, *The Indian Express*, *NDTV* (India), *India Strategic*, *IBNLive* (India), *Business World* (India), Reuters, *Aviation Week*, and The Boeing Company.

## Strong China-Pakistan Security Alignment

Due to India's bitter rivalry with Pakistan, China's friendly relations with Pakistan are a source of tension between China and India. China and Pakistan have enjoyed amicable relations since establishing diplomatic ties in 1951.[47] Chinese and Pakistani officials often describe the bilateral relationship in exceedingly positive terms: "sweeter than honey," "deeper than oceans," and "all-weather friend."[48] Among other objectives, the bilateral relationship serves each country as a means of strategic and military balancing against India.[49] In addition, China's trade and investment ties with Pakistan have been expanding since the late 1990s, with Chinese companies investing in Pakistan's transportation and energy-related infrastructure.[50] China's strong ties with Pakistan affirm the fears of some Indians that China is attempting to encircle India. India is especially concerned about China's support for Pakistan's military through arms sales and technology transfers.

- China is the top exporter of arms to Pakistan. According to the Stockholm International Peace Research Institute (SIPRI), between 2004 and 2013, Pakistan received $4.1 billion in deliveries of Chinese arms, exceeding the $2.7 billion in U.S. arms deliveries during that period.[51] Among the platforms and weapon systems Pakistan procured from China are airborne early warning and control aircraft and missiles and bombs for the JF-17 combat aircraft. Pakistan also acquired Chinese JIANGWEI-class frigates and ship borne surface-to-air and antiship missiles.[52] All of these platforms and weapon systems could be used to challenge the Indian Navy and Air Force in a potential India-Pakistan conflict. China and Pakistan also have been negotiating the sale of six Chinese submarines.[53] If the deal is realized and the submarines are armed with antiship cruise missiles, the submarines would significantly enhance the Pakistan Navy's ability to hold Indian surface ships at risk.

- China-Pakistan defense-industrial cooperation has supported the development of Pakistan's combat aircraft. The Pakistan Air Force has over 30 JF-17 aircraft, which the two countries jointly developed, and it plans to procure more than 150 in total.[54] China and Pakistan also are developing a variant with improved avionics and weapon systems. Pakistan intends for the JF-17 to replace its aging fleet of fighter aircraft.[55]

- China appears to have played a critical role in Pakistan's acquisition of nuclear weapons and ballistic missiles.[56] Beginning in the 1970s, China is reported to have provided Pakistan with support for its nuclear weapons program, including nuclear weapon blueprints, weapons-grade uranium, and various components for the production of a nuclear weapon.[57] In the 1990s, China is reported to also have assisted Pakistan with the development of its Shaheen I short-range ballistic missiles and its Shaheen II medium-range ballistic missiles.[58] These capabilities fundamentally changed the India-Pakistan security relationship, because they provided Pakistan with a deterrent against invasion by the more militarily powerful India.

- China and Pakistan reached a deal in 2013 for China to build two more civil nuclear power plants in Pakistan, which would supplement the two plants that China has already built. The Chinese government argues the deal would not violate its international nonproliferation obligations, but the U.S. and Indian governments have raised concerns about expanded China-Pakistan civil nuclear cooperation.[59]

**Tibet**

Tibet has been a key factor in China-India relations since China's occupation of Tibet in the early 1950s. In March 1959, the 14th Dalai Lama, Tibet's political and spiritual leader, fled to India to avoid the Chinese government's crackdown on a popular armed revolt against Chinese rule in Lhasa, the capital of Tibet. Following the revolt, China established complete military and political control over Tibet.[60] The Dalai Lama established the Central Tibetan Administration, which is commonly referred to as the Tibetan government-in-exile, in Dharamsala, India. The organization's stated goals are "rehabilitating Tibetan refugees and restoring freedom and happiness in Tibet."[61]

The Dalai Lama's presence in India creates tensions in China-India relations.

- Insecure about its control over Tibet, China fears India will use the presence of the Dalai Lama and the large Tibetan refugee population in India to foment unrest in Tibet. China asserts the area it claims in Arunachal Pradesh is part of Tibet.[62]

- The succession of the 79-year old Dalai Lama has the potential to complicate China-India relations. The Dalai Lama has said he might nominate his successor and that he might not even have a successor. The Chinese government, however, holds that only Beijing has the power to select the Dalai Lama.[63]

Another reason Tibet plays an important role in China-India relations is that the Brahmaputra River, one of India's major rivers, begins in the TAR. To generate electricity, China is constructing dams on the river and India plans to do so as well.[64] In November 2014, the first Chinese hydropower dam on the river, one of four the Chinese government plans to build, began partial operation. New Delhi and Beijing have discussed these projects and the Chinese government has stated the dams will not affect downstream areas, but if the dams lead to worsened flooding or lessened water availability in India, this issue could become a major source of tension in bilateral relations.[65]

**India's Trade Imbalance with China**

India's trade imbalance with China is another area of friction in the bilateral relationship. Indian officials have raised this issue with their Chinese counterparts, including the two meetings between Prime Minister Modi and President Xi since Prime Minister Modi's election.[66] India's customs data for fiscal year 2014 (March 2013 to March 2014) show India traded $65.9 billion worth of goods with China, up from $7 billion in fiscal year 2004. Although India's goods exports to China have increased modestly, China still accounts for a larger share of India's imports than its exports. This past year, China contributed one-quarter of India's $138.6 billion trade deficit with the world (see Figure 2).

**Figure 2: India's Goods Trade with the World and the Share of China and the United States**
(US$ billions; share, %)

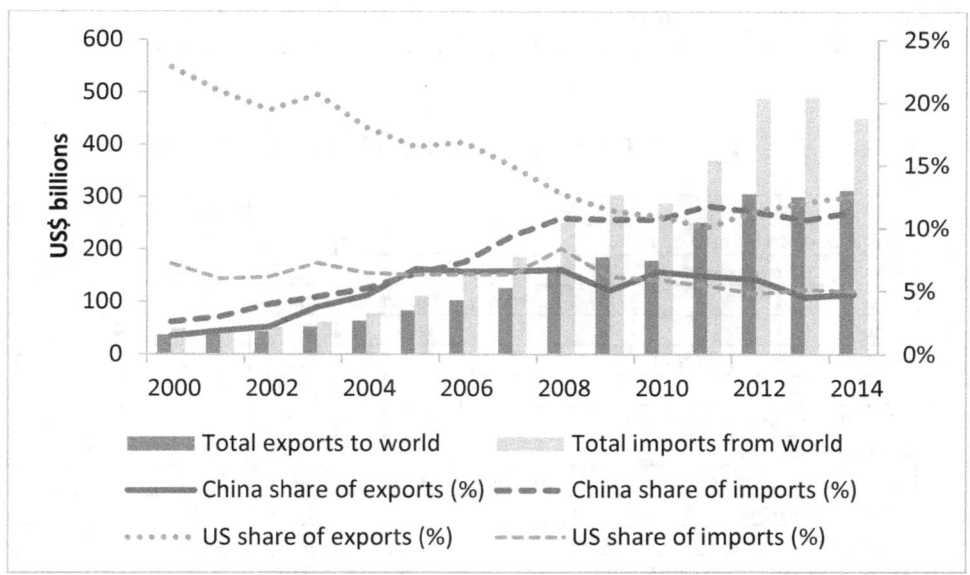

*Sources*: Reserve Bank of India and India's Ministry of Commerce and Industry, via CEIC.
*Note:* Years based on Indian fiscal years, which run from March to March. For example, "2014" denotes March 2013 to March 2014.

To some extent, this trade imbalance is the result of market dynamics. A substantial share of India's imports from China is composed of intermediate inputs used by Indian industry. Between fiscal years 2004 and 2014, India's total chemical imports rose from $4.4 billion to $21.8 billion. During that period, China's share of those chemical imports increased by 17 percentage points, to 45.6 percent. India uses organic chemicals in its export-oriented pharmaceutical industry, which ships increasingly to the U.S. market.[67] Moreover, India is keen to expand labor-intensive manufacturing to promote urbanization and take advantage of its large labor endowment, whereas China is shifting to capital-intensive production.

Despite these factors, the overall composition of bilateral trade seems harmful to India. India's shipments to China consist primarily of raw materials that do little to spur manufacturing activity and technological innovation in the Indian economy. This trend contrasts with China's industrial manufacturing exports to India. India has seen a large rise in its cotton, copper, mineral fuel, and ore shipments to China (see Table 2). In fiscal year 2014, these product lines accounted for 55.8 percent of Indian exports to China and only 25.3 percent of Indian exports to the world.[68] Such products are particularly susceptible to price fluctuations and foreign trade policies. For example, China's decision to reduce cotton stockpiling earlier this year led to a sharp decline in China's purchases of Indian cotton.*

---

[*]China's imports of cotton have increased substantially in recent years. Mark D. Lange, president and CEO of the National Cotton Council, has told the Commission that this is the result of China's procurement policies. In calendar years 2010 and 2011, world cotton prices went through a period of strengthening and volatility, and China saw its total year-end cotton stocks fall to the lowest level in 20 years. Responding to concerns about reserves, in September 2011, China initiated a policy of purchasing cotton into its national reserves, paying 40 to 50 cents above world prices in order to support domestic growers. This policy significantly distorted the world cotton markets. Cotton has become so expensive in China that the yarn industry is finding it economical to import from abroad in excess of China's WTO tariff-rate quota, even though this means paying high import tariffs. In April 2014, however, China suddenly indicated that it would abandon its cotton stockpiling program because it was becoming too costly to sustain. U.S.-China Economic and Security Review Commission, *Hearing on China's Agriculture Policy and U.S. Access to China's Market*, testimony of Mark Lange, April 25, 2013; Meenakshi Sharma, "India's Cotton Exports Hit as China Shifts Policy," Reuters, April 17, 2014. *http://in.reuters.com/article/2014/04/17/india-cotton-exports-idINL4N0MP2MK20140417*.

In parallel, India's imports of Chinese machinery, nuclear reactors, and vehicles have all increased (see Table 2). According to Nasscom, the industry body that represents India's information technology (IT) industry, India exported $75.8 billion worth of IT products in fiscal year 2013, but almost none of these went to China. Nasscom has claimed that China only allows its own companies to operate in the IT sector, as "state-owned enterprises have restrictive conditions on who they work with."[69]

**Table 2: Composition of India's Trade with China**

|  | 1999 | 2004 | 2009 | 2014 |
|---|---|---|---|---|
| Total Exports to China (US$ millions) | 427 | 2,955 | 9,353 | 14,824 |
| Total Imports from China (US$ millions) | 1,097 | 4,053 | 32,497 | 51,034 |
| *Percentage of Exports to China* | | | | |
| Cotton | 9.8% | 3.6% | 4.2% | 25.9% |
| Copper and Articles thereof | 0.0% | 1.2% | 1.3% | 12.4% |
| Ores, Slag, and Ash | 26.1% | 29.3% | 51.5% | 10.6% |
| Mineral Fuels and Mineral Oils | 0.0% | 2.5% | 1.2% | 6.9% |
| Organic Chemicals | 11.0% | 7.5% | 4.3% | 6.2% |
| Salt, Sulphur, Earth and Stones, and Plastering Material | 3.8% | 3.0% | 3.0% | 4.6% |
| Plastic and Articles | 0.3% | 9.0% | 1.6% | 3.8% |
| Nuclear Reactors, Boilers, and Machinery | 2.0% | 2.3% | 2.5% | 3.3% |
| Aircraft, Spacecraft and Parts | 0.0% | 0.0% | 0.0% | 2.8% |
| Iron and Steel | 1.6% | 20.4% | 3.9% | 2.2% |
| Electrical Machinery, Equipment, and Parts | 1.1% | 1.0% | 1.2% | 2.0% |
| All other (< 2% share) | 44.4% | 20.0% | 25.4% | 19.4% |
| *Percentage of Imports from China* | | | | |
| Electrical Machinery, Equipment, and Parts | 10.0% | 29.2% | 30.8% | 27.9% |
| Nuclear Reactors, Boilers, and Machinery | 11.3% | 12.2% | 17.0% | 18.5% |
| Organic Chemicals | 21.2% | 15.9% | 8.7% | 10.6% |
| Project Goods | 4.9% | 0.1% | 3.7% | 4.2% |
| Fertilizers | 0.3% | 0.3% | 2.8% | 3.8% |
| Plastic and Articles | 1.1% | 1.4% | 1.6% | 2.6% |
| Articles of Iron or Steel | 1.0% | 1.1% | 3.2% | 2.4% |
| Optical, Photographic, and Cinematographic Measuring | 1.4% | 1.6% | 1.8% | 2.0% |
| Vehicles excl. Railway, Rolling Stock, and Parts | 0.2% | 0.2% | 1.3% | 1.9% |
| Iron and Steel | 1.9% | 0.5% | 5.3% | 1.9% |
| All other (< 2% share) | 46.6% | 37.6% | 23.9% | 24.2% |

*Source*: India's Ministry of Commerce and Industry, via CEIC.
*Note:* Years based on Indian fiscal years, which run from March to March. For example, "2014" denotes March 2013 to March 2014.

Differences in the two economies point to some of the roots of the bilateral trade deficit. India maintains a large trade deficit with the world, amounting to seven percent of gross domestic product (GDP) in 2012 (see Figure 3). In contrast, China maintains a substantial surplus in its global trade. Although China has agreed to lower import tariffs under the WTO, its domestic producers derive competitive advantages from a litany of non-tariff barriers, including state influence over the financial sector; taxes that promote exports and discourage imports; price controls on energy; laws that restrict collective bargaining; and policies that unfairly advantage state-backed enterprises over private and foreign companies.

**Figure 3: Breakdown of China and India's GDP, 1990 vs. 2012**

(share, %)

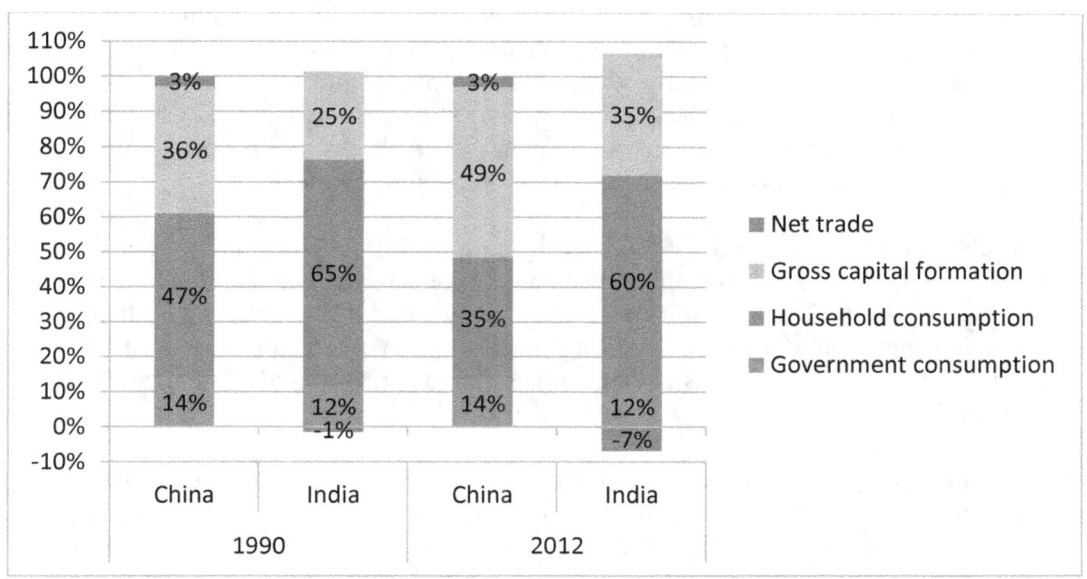

*Source*: World Bank Development Indicators.

Strict capital and currency controls have allowed the People's Bank of China to accumulate nearly $4 trillion in foreign reserves.[70] India, in contrast, suffers from external debts that are not fully covered by its foreign reserves. The Central Bank of India's more liberal monetary policy exposes the country's businesses to external market forces, such as currency fluctuation and changes in lending rates. Strong credit growth has allowed China to invest more heavily than India in infrastructure, including transport logistics. According to the World Bank, exporting a container of goods from China in 2012 cost $580, about half the cost of shipping the same container of goods from India.[71] China is also better connected to global shipping networks.[*] Moreover, comparative data from the World Economic Forum's *Global Trade Enabling Report 2014* show Chinese exporters have easier access to trade finance than their counterparts in India.[72]

In general, China's economy is also larger and more competitive than India's. Thirty years ago, the two countries' economies were approximately equal in size; in 2012, China's GDP was over three times greater than India's.[73] Since their populations are roughly equivalent, China's per capita income has also outgrown India's by a long margin, providing households with more wealth to spend. Moreover, greater market size has allowed China to attract more business activity from foreign companies. China's foreign direct investment (FDI) inflows in 2012 were 11 times higher than India's, allowing it to tap into international expertise, technology, and capital.[†] Due to its onerous regulatory regime, India ranks just 142nd in the World Bank's "Ease of Doing Business" index, fifty-two spots behind China[74] Although Chinese manufacturers lack competitiveness in higher-margin and innovative industries, they have benefited from economies of scale, a large and increasingly skilled labor pool, and the clustering of supply chains. Even in services, where India is generally competitive, China generated greater export revenue in 2012.[75]

---

[*] This assessment is based on the Liner Shipping Connectivity Index, which is derived from five indicators in the maritime transport sector: number of ships, their container-carrying capacity, maximum vessel size, number of services, and number of companies that deploy container ships in a country's ports. In 2012, China scored 144 on the index; India scored only 41. The average for all countries is 100. Data from World Bank Development Indicators.

[†] In 2012, China's primary income on FDI (in current U.S. dollars) was $187.5 billion; India's was $16.4 billion. Data from World Bank Development Indicators.

Going forward, however, development trends in the two countries could lead to India's increased competiveness in the bilateral relationship:

- China's high rates of investment have crowded out household consumption as the main source of economic activity (see Figure 3). Years of capital-intensive growth have precipitated imbalances, resulting in resource waste, excess capacity, and asset bubbles. Although China is a net creditor to the world, the credit in its domestic economy—much of it in opaque "shadow banking" instruments—has become a serious risk. Although India's economic structure is not optimal either, it is less skewed toward credit-driven investment.

- With regard to demographics, China is aging quickly; by 2040, one in four Chinese will be over age 65—a total of 300 million people.[76] China's median age is 35.7, nine years older than India's. [77] While China's One-Child Policy has inverted its age pyramid, India is ushering in a young generation of workers. A young workforce can adapt quickly to a changing economy, raise India's competitiveness in labor-intensive industries, and increase the ratio of workers to dependents.

- India is superior to China in terms of its energy efficiency and resource endowments. In 2012, it generated about $7.70 of GDP per kilogram of oil equivalent; China's economy managed just $4.90.[*] China applies four times more fertilizer per hectare of arable land than India, compounding the environmental damage to increasingly scarce arable land.[78]

- Concerns about rule of law, availability of information, and regime stability make China a potentially more volatile and inhospitable economic environment than India. India shares problems with China, such as bureaucratic inefficiency, corruption, and violations of intellectual property, but, over time, India's clear separation of powers, constitutional rights, and electoral process could make it an attractive alternative for foreign businesses in comparison to China's authoritarian model.

# Areas of Cooperation

Despite the tension in China-India relations, the two countries seek to cooperate on a variety of issues. Bilateral and multilateral cooperation helps to soften the effects of the areas of tension on China-India relations.[79]

While visiting India in May 2013, Chinese premier Li Keqiang said, "Both [then prime minister Manmohan Singh] and I believe there are far more interests than differences between our two sides. We need to confront issues with a broad mind, and tackle them in a mature way."[80] In September 2014, on the first day of President Xi's trip to India, *The Hindu* published an op-ed by President Xi in which he wrote:

> *"The combination of the world's factory and the world's back office will produce the most competitive production base ... We need to connect our development strategies more closely and jointly pursue our common dream of national strength and prosperity ... I look forward to an in-depth exchange of views with Indian leaders on our bilateral relations during the visit, and to injecting new vitality to our strategic and cooperative partnership for peace and prosperity."[81]*

---

[*] Measured in constant 2011 purchasing power parity. Data from World Bank Development Indicators.

During President Xi's visit, Prime Minister Modi also expressed his hopes for the relationship. He said, "In the last two days, in Ahmedabad and Delhi we talked about all aspects of India-China relations. We have decided to increase cooperation on every possible front."[82]

One area of developing bilateral cooperation is stability in Afghanistan. Afghanistan was a topic of discussion between the two heads of state during President Xi's visit, building upon a formal dialogue mechanism regarding Afghanistan that China and India established in April 2013.[83] With India's upcoming accession to the Shanghai Cooperation Organization (SCO), New Delhi and Beijing will be discussing Afghanistan in this forum as well. The SCO, which currently includes China, Russia, Kazakhstan, Kyrgyzstan, Tajikistan, and Uzbekistan as permanent members, focuses on security and economic cooperation and is concerned about the stability of nearby Afghanistan.

China and India also have been cooperating on climate change issues, building on a bilateral memorandum of understanding signed in 2009. In their joint statement in September 2014 President Xi and Prime Minister Modi recognized the need to "achieve a balanced, comprehensive and equitable agreement under the UN Framework Convention on Climate Change in 2015."[84] They also agreed to create a joint working group for climate change policy coordination.[85] It is unclear how, if at all, the climate change agreement reached between China and the United States in November 2014 will impact China-India cooperation on this issue.

Moreover, bilateral trade has grown exponentially over the last decade, and both sides hope to strengthen the economic relationship. Initiatives for economic cooperation featured prominently during the Modi-Xi summit in September 2014. Two of the most important agreements involved Chinese investment in India, an effort by China to respond to India's concerns about imbalances in the trade relationship. China pledged to invest $20 billion in two industrial parks in the western states of Gujarat and Maharashtra.[86] The two sides also concluded a cooperation agreement on railway development in India. As part of the agreement, Chinese companies will help India modernize its rail system by improving the capacity of rail tracks to support increased train speeds.[87] This plan effectively involves India in China's far-reaching effort to expand and modernize rail networks domestically and abroad.

New Delhi has become more receptive to Chinese FDI into India, provided it contributes value to priority sectors, such as infrastructure. Keen to generate higher returns on its dollar reserves, China has become an aggressive outbound investor in recent years. Yet, according to India's Department of Industrial Policy and Promotion, China sent just $68 million worth of FDI to India in 2013, accounting for 0.3 percent of India's total FDI inflows. Additional Chinese capital may be entering via Mauritius, Singapore, and Hong Kong—offshore financial centers that have fewer capital controls than mainland China. But it is safe to say China ranks well behind India's top foreign investors, including Japan (6.4 percent) and the United States (3.5 percent).[88]* Weaknesses in Indian infrastructure, coupled with China's capacity for outbound investment, make this an area with great potential for bilateral cooperation.

Other key economic and trade-related outcomes of the Modi-Xi summit included plans to strengthen economic dialogue mechanisms and tentative agreements to increase market integration and regulatory coherence.

- The two sides agreed to strengthen the China-India Strategic Economic Dialogue, which convenes high-level officials to coordinate overall economic policy. The Strategic Economic Dialogue's future emphasis will be on "crosscutting fields" that combine economic cooperation with infrastructure development and resource sustainability. China and India also agreed to hold several other meetings among relevant economic agencies, including (1) the seventh meeting of the India-

---

* China's FDI inflows are difficult to disaggregate, as 62 percent of inflows originate in Hong Kong. China's Ministry of Commerce states that India accounted for 0.2 percent of "FDI utilized" in China last year. *Source*: China's Ministry of Commerce, via CEIC.

China Financial Dialogue, a bilateral forum to enhance financial regulatory cooperation; and (2) a new dialogue between India's Department of Economic Affairs and the Development Research Center of China's State Council to study joint challenges in managing economic rebalancing. In addition, the two sides agreed to further strive to implement the outcomes from the first meeting of a joint study group on the Bangladesh-China-India-Myanmar Economic Corridor, an initiative to enhance infrastructure links, economic and environmental cooperation, and people-to-people contact between the four countries.[89]

- With respect to enforceable outcomes, the summit rendered fewer results. As part of the India-China Financial Dialogue, India agreed "in principle" to allow the Bank of China to open a branch in Mumbai. The two countries also agreed to jointly develop energy-efficient "smart cities," without articulating any specifics. They stated they would cooperate on food and drug issues, particularly registration of pharmaceutical products and speedier phytosanitary negotiations on agricultural goods for two-way trade. Finally, China stated its "willingness" to relax its quota system on imported films to allow more imports of Indian productions, a preliminary step that could pave the way for an increase in bilateral services trade.[90]

In addition to bilateral cooperation, China and India are working together in multilateral forums. At this year's BRICS summit, the five member countries agreed to establish a development bank which is seen as a potential competitor to the World Bank. Another potential avenue of cooperation is the Asian Infrastructure Investment Bank (AIIB), which could come to rival the Asian Development Bank as a source of funding for Asian infrastructure projects. The AIIB's members signed a memorandum on the creation of the bank in October 2014. U.S. allies Australia, Japan, and South Korea did not join, but India was among the signatories. China is expected to be the largest contributor of funding and the largest shareholder in both of these banks, so it remains to be seen how influential India can be in shaping their agendas.[91] In August 2014, officials from China and India also met with counterparts from Brazil and South Africa to discuss climate change policy, one of several meetings the four countries have held on the topic since 2009.[92] Furthermore, Chinese, Indian, and Russian officials have been meeting to discuss stability in Afghanistan.[93]

---

**Energy Competition and Cooperation in China-India Relations**

As emerging economies, China and India strive to meet their rising energy needs while also reducing the environmental damage caused by fossil fuel consumption. These efforts lead to competition as well as cooperation.

China and India are among the world's top five oil consumers and fastest-growing oil and gas importers. They are beginning to shape energy price trends, which historically have been determined by advanced economies.[94] Although China imports a larger volume of oil, India is more import-reliant (see Table 3). The two countries also are importing increasing volumes of liquefied natural gas (LNG). Some experts predict that as India industrializes and urbanizes, its oil and gas imports will grow at a faster rate than China's. China is undergoing a structural shift away from industry and its economic growth has slowed. China may also increase offshore oil and onshore shale gas production, a policy priority outlined in the government's recent Energy Development Strategy Action Plan for 2014-2020.[95]

---

**Table 3: Oil and Gas Consumption in the United States and Major Asian Countries, 2012**

| | Oil consumption | | Gas consumption | |
|---|---|---|---|---|
| | Net import reliance | Share of world | Net import reliance | Share of world |
| United States | 39.9% | 20.7% | 12.3% | 21.4% |
| **China** | **55.7%** | **11.1%** | **28.4%** | **4.3%** |
| **India** | **71.3%** | **3.9%** | **29.0%** | **1.7%** |
| Japan | 97.1% | 5.3% | 93.0% | 3.9% |
| Korea | 97.4% | 2.6% | 95.7% | 1.5% |

*Source:* U.S. Energy Information Administration.

Meanwhile, Chinese and Indian national oil companies are competing for equity oil investment overseas. For example, the exit of Western oil majors from Venezuela following "re-nationalization" policies in 2006 presented an opportunity for Indian and Chinese companies to step in. Indian companies have secured two exploration projects and have also signed contracts to purchase oil through Venezuela for Indian refineries. China has been more aggressive, combining exploration rights, heavy investment in energy infrastructure, and $50 billion worth of energy-backed loans to Venezuela's government.[96] Elsewhere in Latin America, Indian and Chinese companies are also competing in Brazil, the site of the world's largest offshore oil discoveries. Indian company Oil and Natural Gas Company Ltd. (ONGC) joined Shell in 2013 to preempt the purchase of a 35-percent stake in a Brazilian offshore oil field by Sinochem, China's largest chemical producer.[97] According to Indian media reports, "An earlier attempt by ONGC to buy ConocoPhillips' 8.4 percent stake in Kazakhstan's Kashagan offshore oil field was scuttled by China, with the Kazakhstan government exercising its rights to buy the shares on offer. It was later sold off to China."[98]

As part of its "new silk road"* strategy, the Obama Administration has advocated a Turkmenistan-Afghanistan-Pakistan-India pipeline network. The project, if completed, could help India diversify its energy mix by providing an alternative to increasingly expensive seaborne LNG imports. The pipeline also could diversify the destinations for Turkmenistan's gas exports beyond China and Russia to include India. However, there is now little confidence the project can materialize. One challenge is the lack of mutual trust among the four countries involved. Private investors also find Afghanistan too politically unstable to serve as a gas transit hub. European governments, seeking an alternative to Russian supply, may also oppose the pipeline if it means Europe has less access to future supplies of Turkmen gas.[99]

China and India face similar energy dilemmas. They each have abundant coal reserves, but this fuel source can have a devastating impact on public health and the environment.† Both countries are in the process of

---

* According to the U.S. Department of State, "The New Silk Road initiative was first envisioned in 2011 as a means for Afghanistan to integrate further into the region by resuming traditional trading routes and reconstructing significant infrastructure links broken by decades of conflict." The initiative comprises regional energy market integration (especially electricity grid infrastructure), trade and transport (e.g., WTO accession for Afghanistan and Kazakhstan, rehabilitation of roads), customs and border operations (to make customs procedures more efficient but also better able to prevent the transit of weapons, drugs, and human trafficking), and exchange programs for businesses and people (e.g., Central Asia-Afghanistan Women's Economic Symposium). U.S. Department of State, "U.S. Support for the New Silk Road." *http://www.state.gov/p/sca/ci/af/newsilkroad/.*

† Compounding the reliance on thermal energy is the low quality of coal in China and India. China ranks third in global reserves of subbituminous coal, while high-ash bituminous coals are particularly prevalent in India. International Energy Agency Clean Coal Center, "Profiles: Global Perspective on the Use of Low Quality Coals," No. 11/2 (Paris, France: International Energy Agency, April 2011). *http://www.iea-coal.org.uk/documents/82615/7953/Global-perspective-on-the-use-of-low-quality-coals-CCC/180.*

pursuing other sources of clean and renewable energy. For example, in the wind energy sector, Chinese turbine maker Goldwind Science & Technology Co. Ltd. and Indian turbine maker Suzlon Energy Ltd. are competing with leading Western companies such as General Electric. In addition, China's second-largest manufacturer of wind turbines, Ming Yang Wind Power Group Ltd., is aggressively expanding into the Indian market.[100]

At the Modi-Xi Summit, the two sides agreed to carry out bilateral cooperation in civil nuclear energy, including holding working level consultations between the Department of Atomic Energy of India and the China Atomic Energy Authority.[101] Since the 2011 Fukushima Daichi nuclear disaster in Japan, there have been concerns about the safety of nuclear energy, but Beijing and New Delhi appear determined to build new nuclear power stations nonetheless.

# Implications and Opportunities for the United States

The election of Prime Minister Modi, India's evolving strategic calculations, and the growing Indian economy and role in global energy markets have important implications for U.S. security and economic interests and may present opportunities for greater U.S.-India cooperation.

Prime Minister Modi has shown support for the U.S.-India Defense Trade and Technology Initiative (DTTI), an initiative that supports efforts for defense technology co-development and co-production, priorities for India as it seeks to build its indigenous defense industry. The two sides held the initiative's first meeting in September 2014. Subsequently, the joint statement of Prime Minister Modi and President Obama during Prime Minister Modi's visit to the United States in September endorsed the DTTI's creation of a new task force to decide the technologies and projects for which the United States and India will engage in co-development and co-production.[102]

Furthermore, the Modi Administration's proposed increase in defense spending, due in part to China's military modernization, could be a boon for the U.S. defense industry as India seeks to upgrade its military systems and platforms, acquire new capabilities, and strengthen its relationship with the United States.[103]

Nevertheless, U.S. defense firms will continue to face two primary challenges in India: (1) a complex defense procurement bureaucracy; and (2) a highly competitive market due to India's existing relationships with other foreign arms suppliers, particularly Russia, France, and Israel.

- According to S. Amer Latif, former director for South Asian affairs in the Office of South and Southeast Asian Affairs in the U.S. Office of the Undersecretary of Defense for Policy: "The challenge for Americans is getting an element of predictability on when decisions will be made [by the Indian government] to be able to do long-range business planning. The lack of transparency on how and when decisions will be made on defense deals constitutes a major concern for U.S. firms seeking to project costs for bidding on tenders."[104] Other problems with the Indian defense procurement bureaucracy include the insufficient number of defense procurement officials, the high turnover and low level of defense acquisition experience among these officials, and centralized decision-making that slows the procurement process.[105]

- India imports the vast majority of its defense equipment from Russia. Of the $25 billion in defense equipment delivered to India between 2004 and 2013, Russian products accounted for a 74 percent share, according to SIPRI.[106] In contrast, deliveries of U.S. products made up only six percent of India's imports of defense equipment during that time.[107] However, India has signed major deals with U.S. defense companies in recent years, including deals for six C-130J transport aircraft, 10

C-17A transport aircraft, and eight P-8I maritime patrol aircraft.[108] Going forward, India may procure U.S.-made heavy lift and attack helicopters.[109]

The Modi Administration has also raised the cap on FDI in the defense sector from 26 percent to 49 percent. However, because foreign investors in India's defense sector will still lack a controlling share of their investments, the positive effects of this policy for U.S. defense companies will be limited.[110]

India probably would support more robust bilateral training and security activities with the United States in areas such as humanitarian assistance and disaster relief, search and rescue, noncombatant evacuation, maritime reconnaissance patrol, counterterrorism, counterpiracy, and counterproliferation.[111] Moreover, while the U.S. Army, Navy, and Air Force conduct training and exchanges with their Indian counterparts, there are no institutionalized strategic dialogue mechanisms between them. India may be open to establishing such a mechanism to facilitate broader cooperation and collaboration in areas of mutual interest such as counterinsurgency, stability in Afghanistan, and Chinese military developments.[112]

Despite the potential for enhanced military and security activities, India likely will continue to balance its desire to partner with the United States with its longstanding goal of "strategic autonomy" and its concern that closer U.S.-India ties could antagonize China and upset India-China relations.[113] Furthermore, concerns about the United States' reliability and memories of U.S. sanctions on India after its nuclear tests in the late 1990s hamper Indian officials' trust in the United States. Some Indian officials are also concerned a stronger U.S.-India security relationship would be unequal, with India playing the role of a junior partner.[114]

India's growing perception of China as a threat is driving New Delhi to strengthen military ties with some U.S. allies and associates in the Asia Pacific region,[*] including Australia, Japan, South Korea, and Vietnam. India also may be motivated to develop closer security relations with other countries in the region to hedge against a potential decline in U.S. military and economic influence and to avoid being overly dependent on Washington for its regional security needs.

- In the past decade, India has significantly expanded its defense partnerships with countries in the Asia Pacific region, primarily through increased participation in bilateral and multilateral military exercises. After signing an upgraded Defense Cooperation Agreement in 2003, India and Singapore have held regular joint military exercises.[115] India and Japan began conducting bilateral exercises in 2012 and Japan joined the U.S.-India Malabar exercise in 2009, 2011, and 2014.[116] India and Australia are planning their first bilateral maritime exercise in 2015. Additionally, India has taken a leading role in training Southeast Asian navies, particularly those of Burma and Vietnam.[117]

- India is increasing its defense equipment cooperation with other countries in the Asia Pacific region. In October 2014, India agreed to sell maritime patrol ships to Vietnam and the two countries are discussing a possible sale of India's BrahMos cruise missile.[118] A year prior, India's Ministry of Defense approved a contract to purchase eight minesweeper ships from Kangnam, a South Korean company.[119] Moreover, the governments of India and Japan are discussing the potential transfer of Japanese US-2 amphibious aircraft to India.[120]

Incrementally expanding security cooperation between India and U.S. allies and associates in the region could further promote U.S. security objectives and augment the U.S. rebalance to the Asia Pacific region.

---

[*] U.S. treaty allies in the Asia Pacific region are Australia, Japan, the Philippines, South Korea, and Thailand. Established and emerging U.S. security associates are India, Indonesia, Malaysia, New Zealand, Singapore, Taiwan, and Vietnam.

- Such cooperation has the potential to strengthen Indian military capabilities while allowing India to avoid being tied too closely to the United States, one of India's priorities and a factor that limits U.S.-India defense cooperation.

- Increased military exercises among U.S. regional allies and associates could improve each country's ability and willingness to contribute to multilateral military activities such as humanitarian assistance and disaster relief. For the U.S. military, humanitarian assistance and disaster relief is one of its most important missions in the Asia Pacific region. In testimony to Congress, Admiral Samuel Locklear, Commander of U.S. Pacific Command, said, "The Indo-Asia-Pacific region is the world's most disaster-prone with 80 percent of all natural disaster occurrences. It contends with more super-typhoons, cyclones, tsunamis, earthquakes, and floods than any other region."[121]

- Acquisition of and training on some common weapon systems and platforms could increase interoperability between India and U.S. allies and associates—as well as between India and the U.S. military.[122] India's training with close U.S. allies such as Australia, Japan, and South Korea also could help to reinforce the use of (or at least familiarity with) U.S.-compatible tactics, techniques, and procedures. Developing interoperability with U.S. allies and associates may be less sensitive for the Indian government and military than doing so with the United States.[123]

- Improved military capabilities and security cooperation among U.S. allies and associates could help each country better respond to Chinese military activities and address capability shortcomings or vulnerabilities. These advances also could cause Beijing to more closely consider the costs of launching a military operation against any one of them.[124]

Finally, in the economic realm, through cooperation with India, the United States has an opportunity to promote a greater balance of economic power in the Asia Pacific region, encourage greater market access in China, promote China's compliance with its WTO obligations, and contribute to global energy security.

- The United States is a growing destination for Indian goods and services exports, and India has used these exports to reduce its trade deficit with the world. The United States could develop this commercial relationship by engaging with India more directly in other areas, such as research cooperation, bilateral investment, and financial sector integration. Efforts by the United States to support India's economic growth could lead to a more balanced distribution of economic power in the Asia Pacific region.

- The United States and India have a common interest in improving market access and WTO compliance in China. Both countries are pursuing these goals in their bilateral relations with China through various dialogue mechanisms such as the U.S.-China Joint Commission on Commerce and Trade and the China-India Strategic Economic Dialogue.

- The United States and India also have cooperated in the WTO to address these challenges. In July 2012, India, along with seven other WTO members, acted as a third-party complainant in the United States' complaint against China's antidumping and countervailing duties on U.S. automobile exports. In December 2012 and June 2013, India and the United States acted as third-party complainants in Japan and the European Union's complaints against China's anti-dumping duties on high-performance stainless steel seamless tubes.* More such coordination could be beneficial to

---

* The cases referenced are DS440, DS454, and DS460.

Washington and New Delhi, since the joint actions of large economies can reduce China's leverage in the WTO.

- The gradual shift of global oil consumption from the United States to Asia will have a deep impact on energy markets and geopolitics in the decades to come. The Organization of the Petroleum Exporting Countries (OPEC), which accounts for roughly two-fifths of global oil supply, has primarily based its production decisions on the U.S. market. However, it is beginning to consider Indian and Chinese demand. The United States, China, and India have a mutual interest in mitigating OPEC's influence over oil prices. The United States could advocate for Indian and Chinese accession to the International Energy Agency (IEA). The IEA coordinates emergency oil-sharing arrangements at the multilateral level but will become less effective if it continues to exclude large emerging economies, like China and India, from its deliberations. The United States could also encourage China and India, along with Japan and South Korea, to better coordinate their purchases and stockpiling of oil and gas.

[1] Open Source Center, *China-India Economic Relations at a Glance*, September 13, 2013. OSC ID: CHO2013091326108110; K. Alan Kronstadt, *India's New Government and Implications for U.S. Interests* (Congressional Research Service, August 2014).

[2] Jonathan Holsag, *China and India: Prospects for Peace* (New York, NY: Columbia University Press, 2010), pp.44-46.

[3] Tanvi Madan, "The Modi-Xi Summit and China-India Relations." (Washington, DC: The Brookings Institution, September 16, 2014). *http://www.brookings.edu/research/opinions/2014/09/16-modi-xi-summit-and-china-india-relations.*

[4] Gardiner Harris, "India and China Vow to Cooperate on Border," *New York Times*, May 20, 2013. *http://www.nytimes.com/2013/05/21/world/asia/india-china-border-issues.html?*; China Ministry of Foreign Affairs, *Foreign Ministry Spokesperson Hua Chunying's Regular Press Conference on April 25, 2013*, April 27, 2013. OSC ID: CPP20130427968070; Open Source Center, *Summary: India Protests PRC Troop 'Intrusion,'* April 23, 2013. OSC ID: FEA20130423030877; Andrew North, "Premier Li Keqiang's Visit: India and China in Border Row Pledge," BBC, May 20, 2013. *http://www.bbc.com/news/world-asia-india-22592770;* Xi Jinping, "Towards an Asian century of prosperity," *Hindu*, September 17, 2014. *http://www.thehindu.com/todays-paper/tp-opinion/towards-an-asian-century-of-prosperity/article6417277.ece.*

[5] C. Raja Mohan, *Samudra Manthan: Sino-Indian Rivalry in the Indian Pacific* (Washington, DC: Carnegie Endowment for International Peace, 2012), pp. 16, 32.

[6] John W. Garver, *Protracted Contest: Sino-Indian Rivalry in the Twentieth Century* (Seattle, WA, University of Washington Press, 2001), pp. 80, 97, 192; John W. Garver, "China's Decision for War with India in 1962," in Alastair Iain Johnston and Robert S. Ross eds., *New Directions in the Study of China's Foreign Policy* (Stanford, CA, Stanford University Press, 2006), pp. 122-123; M. Taylor Fravel, *Strong Borders, Secure Nation: Cooperation and Conflict in China's Territorial Disputes* (Princeton, NJ, Princeton University Press, 2008), pp.196, 198.

[7] Alyssa Ayers, "China's Mixed Messages to India," *Asia Unbound* (Council on Foreign Relations Blog), September 17, 2014. *http://blogs.cfr.org/asia/2014/09/17/chinas-mixed-messages-to-india/*; Open Source Center, *Summary: India Protests PRC Troop 'Intrusion'*, April 23, 2013. OSC ID: FEA20130423030877.

[8] Shishir Gupta, "China, India in Border Skirmish ahead of Xi Visit," *Hindustan Times* (India), September 15, 2014. *http://www.hindustantimes.com/india-news/chinese-civilians-intrude-into-ladakh-area/article1-1264293.aspx.*

[9] *Economic Times* (India), "Incursion by China during President Xi's Visit 'Uncommon': Indo-Tibetan Border Police," October 22, 2014. *http://articles.economictimes.indiatimes.com/2014-10-22/news/55318994_1_itbp-president-xi-jinping-chinese-president*; Shannon Tiezzi, "China, India End Military Stand-Off along Disputed Border," *Diplomat*, October 1, 2014. *http://thediplomat.com/2014/10/china-india-end-military-stand-off-along-disputed-border/.*

[10] M. Taylor Fravel, "China Views India's Rise: Deepening Cooperation, Managing Differences," in Ashley Tellis, Travis Tanner, and Jessica Keogh eds. *Asia Responds to its Rising Powers: China and India* (Seattle, WA, National Bureau of Asian Research, 2011), p. 90.

[11] Open Source Center, *JFJB: Chengdu MAC Troops Explore Fighting and Training Methods for Highland Joint Operations*, August 2014. OSC ID: CPP20120816702004.

[12] *Economist*, "The Communist Party Deepens Tibet's Integration with the Rest of the Country," June 21, 2014. *http://www.economist.com/news/china/21604594-communist-party-deepens-tibets-integration-rest-country-taming-west*; Ananth Krishnan, "China Opens New Highway near Arunachal Pradesh Border," *Hindu*, November 1, 2013. *http://www.thehindu.com/news/international/world/china-opens-new-highway-near-arunachal-pradesh-border/article5302068.ece.*

[13] Rajat Pandit, "With Eye on China, India Deploys Akash Missiles in Northeast," *Times of India*, August 22, 2014. *http://timesofindia.indiatimes.com/india/With-eye-on-China-India-deploys-Akash-missiles-in-northeast/articleshow/40645978.cms.*

[14] Syed Nazakat, "India Scales up Military Forces on Disputed China Border," *Christian Science Monitor*, May 21, 2014. *http://www.csmonitor.com/World/Asia-South-Central/2014/0521/India-scales-up-military-forces-on-disputed-China-border.*

[15] *NDTV* (India), "India holds military exercises close to China border," March 1, 2012. *http://www.ndtv.com/article/india/india-holds-military-exercises-close-to-china-border-181633.*

[16] Rajeev Sharma, "India Ups the Ante along Chinese Border," *Diplomat*, August 22, 2012. *http://thediplomat.com/2012/08/india-ups-the-ante-along-chinese-border/.*

[17] Press Trust of India, "India Announces 54 New Outposts in Arunachal Despite Border Dispute with China," October 24, 2014. *http://www.firstpost.com/india/india-announces-54-new-outposts-arunachal-despite-border-dispute-china-1771315.html*; Tommy Wilkes, "With Eye on China, Modi's India Plans to Develop Disputed Border Region," Reuters, September 14, 2014. *http://www.businessinsider.com/r-with-eye-on-china-modis-india-to-develop-disputed-border-region-2014-9*; Vishwa Mohan and Rajat Pandit, "Defence Projects along LAC to Get Quick Green Nod," *Times of India*, June 13, 2014. *http://timesofindia.indiatimes.com/india/Defence-projects-along-LAC-to-get-quick-green-nod/articleshow/36455655.cms.*

[18] Open Source Center, *Indian Article Examines Need for Strong Defense Infrastructure Along China Border*, March 2012. OSC ID: SAP20120407513030; Open Source Center, *India: Minister Reveals Government Plans To Build 2000 Km Border Road in Arunachal Pradesh*, October 2014. OSC ID: SAO2014101621649261.

[19] U.S.-China Economic and Security Review Commission, *Hearing on China's Maritime Disputes in the East and South China Seas*, testimony of Lloyd Thrall, April 4, 2013; Andrew Erickson and Lyle Goldstein, "Gunboats for China's New 'Grand

Canals'? Probing the Intersection of Beijing's Naval and Oil Security Policies," *Naval War College Review* Vol. 62 No. 2 (Spring 2008).

[20] Andrew Erickson and Austin Strange, *No Substitute for Experience: Chinese Antipiracy Operations in the Gulf of Aden* (Newport, RI: China Maritime Studies Institute, November 2013); U.S.-China Economic and Security Review Commission, *2013 Annual Report to Congress* (Washington, DC: November 2013), pp. 305-306; and U.S.-China Economic and Security Review Commission, *Hearing on China and the Middle East and North Africa,* testimony of Andrew Erickson, June 6, 2013.

[21] Chen Guangshun, "The Survey Ship 'Ocean-1' Smoothly Completes Sea Trials in the South Sea," *China Ocean News*, November 18, 2013. OSC ID: CHR2013111868770077; U.S. Department of Defense, *Annual Report to Congress on Military and Security Developments Involving the People's Republic of China 2013* (Washington, DC: May 2013), p. 39; and Senate Armed Services Committee, *Hearing on U.S. Pacific Command Posture*, testimony of Admiral Samuel J. Locklear, 113th Cong., March 5, 2013.

[22] Kyle Mizokami, "These 5 Ships Are the Real Future of the Chinese Navy," *Foreign Policy*, December 16, 2013. *http://complex.foreignpolicy.com/posts/2013/12/16/these_five_ships_are_the_real_future_of_the_chinese_navy*; Zee News, "Chinese Ship Caught Spying on India," August 31, 2011. *http://zeenews.india.com/news/world/chinese-ship-caught-spying-on-india_729165.html*; Mark Valencia, "Intelligence Gathering, the South China Sea, and the Law of the Sea," Nautilus Institute for Security and Sustainability Policy Forum 11-28, August 30, 2011. *http://nautilus.org/napsnet/napsnet-policy-forum/intelligence-gathering-the-south-china-sea-and-the-law-of-the-sea/*; Peter Dutton, *Scouting, Signaling, and Gatekeeping: Chinese Naval Operations in Japanese Waters and the International Law Implications* (Newport, RI: U.S. Naval War College, February 2009), p. 3.

[23] *China's Navy Extends its Combat Reach to the Indian Ocean* (U.S.-China Economic and Security Review Commission, March 14, 2014). *http://origin.www.uscc.gov/sites/default/files/Research/Staff%20Report_China%27s%20Navy%20Extends%20its%20Combat%20Reach%20to%20the%20Indian%20Ocean.pdf*

[24] Sandeep Unnithan, "Exclusive: Indian Navy Headless as Chinese Nuclear Sub Prowls Indian Ocean," *India Today*, March 21, 2014. *http://indiatoday.intoday.in/story/indian-navy-chinese-nuclear-sub-indian-ocean/1/350498.html*; Senate Armed Services Committee, *Defense Intelligence Agency Annual Threat Assessment*, written statement of Michael Flynn, February 11, 2014. p. 28. *http://www.armed-services.senate.gov/imo/media/doc/Flynn_02-11-14.pdf*.

[25] Sandeep Unnithan, " 'Hidden Dragon' on the High Seas: China's Deployment of Nuclear-Powered Attack Submarine," *Fortuna's Corner*, March 21, 2014. *http://fortunascorner.com/2014/04/01/hidden-dragon-on-high-seas-chinas-deployment-of-nuclear-powered-attack-submarine/*.

[26] *Colombo Gazette*, "Chinese Submarine Docks in Sri Lanka," November 2, 2014. *http://colombogazette.com/2014/11/02/chinese-submarine-docks-in-sri-lanka/*.

[27] Anusha Ondaatije, "Sri Lanka Opens $500 Million Port Terminal Built by China," Bloomberg, August 5, 2013. *http://www.bloomberg.com/news/2013-08-04/sri-lanka-to-open-500-million-container-terminal-built-by-china.html*; Sri Lanka Ports Authority, "Development of Port in Hambantota." *http://www.slpa.lk/port_hambantota.asp?chk=4*.

[28] Gwadar Port Authority, *"Chairman's Message." http://www.gwadarport.gov.pk/home.html*.

[29] Andrew Erickson and Austin Strange, *No Substitute for Experience: Chinese Antipiracy Operations in the Gulf of Aden* (Newport, RI: China Maritime Studies Institute, November 2013).

[30] Open Source Center, *Some Indian Officials, Media Concerned Over Losing Clout to PRC*, December 22, 2012. OSC ID: SAP20121222534003; C. Raja Mohan, *Samudra Manthan: Sino-Indian Rivalry in the Indian Pacific* (Washington, DC: Carnegie Endowment for International Peace, 2012), p. 40.

[31] *India Strategic*, "Maritime Security of India Future Challenges," December 2013. OSC ID: SAL2014010741528940; Niharika Mandhana and Josh Chin, "India Launches Homegrown Aircraft Carrier," *Wall Street Journal*, August 12, 2013. *http://online.wsj.com/news/articles/SB10001424127887324085304579008540915051228*; C. Raja Mohan, *Samudra Manthan: Sino-Indian Rivalry in the Indian Pacific* (Washington, DC: Carnegie Endowment for International Peace, 2012), p. 61; *Asian Military Review*, "India Strengthen Coastal Security Network," August 27, 2012. *http://www.asianmilitaryreview.com/india-strengthen-coastal-security-network/*; and *Asian News International*, "India aiming for real-time maritime domain awareness: Antony," October 25, 2010. *http://in.news.yahoo.com/india-aiming-real-time-maritime-domain-awareness-antony.html*.

[32] Alan Kronstadt and Sonia Pinto, *U.S.-India Security Relations: Strategic Issues* (Congressional Research Service, January 2013), pp. 10, 29.

[33] Sujan Dutta, "Wargames End, Minus Mishap," *Telegraph* (India), March 1, 2014. *http://www.telegraphindia.com/1140302/jsp/nation/story_18036892.jsp#.VElhS_nF-Sp*; Rajat Pandit, "Navy Kicks off Largest Combat Exercise with Dedicated Satellite Above," February 13, 2014. Times of India. *http://timesofindia.indiatimes.com/india/Navy-kicks-off-largest-combat-exercise-with-dedicated-satellite-above/articleshow/30349037.cms*.

[34] Rahul Bedi, "India Commissions First-of-Class Destroyer Kolkata," *Jane's IHS*, August 18, 2014. *http://www.janes.com/article/42106/india-commissions-first-of-class-destroyer-kolkata*.

[35] Manu Pubby, "Navy Seals 45,000-cr Deal: Seven Warships," *Indian Express*, June 20, 2009. *http://archive.indianexpress.com/news/navy-seals-45-000-cr-deal--seven-warships/479132*.

[36] Vivek Raghuvanshi, "Indian Navy Wants to Fast-Track Purchase of Russian Subs," *Defense News*, August 2, 2014. *http://www.defensenews.com/article/20140802/DEFREG03/308020016/Indian-Navy-Wants-Fast-Track-Purchase-Russian-Subs*.

[37] Pallava Bagla and Vishnu Som, "NDTV Exclusive: This is INS Arihant, First Made-in-India Nuclear Submarine," *NDTV* (India), August 20, 2014. *http://www.ndtv.com/article/india/ndtv-exclusive-this-is-ins-arihant-first-made-in-india-nuclear-submarine-578949.*

[38] Vivek Raghuvanshi, "Indian Navy Wants to Fast-Track Purchase of Russian Subs," *Defense News*, August 2, 2014. *http://www.defensenews.com/article/20140802/DEFREG03/308020016/Indian-Navy-Wants-Fast-Track-Purchase-Russian-Subs.*

[39] Open Source Center, *Article Analyzes India's Strategic Challenges in Developing Naval Power, Enhancing Maritime Security,* December 1, 2013. OSC ID: SAL2014010741528940.

[40] Saurav Jha, "The India Navy's Quest for Amphibious Assault Ships," *IBNLive* (India), October 24, 2014. *http://ibnlive.in.com/blogs/sauravjha/2976/65411/the-indian-navys-quest-for-amphibious-assault-ships.html.*

[41] Boeing, "Boeing Delivers 6th P-8I Maritime Patrol Aircraft to India," November 25, 2014. *http://boeing.mediaroom.com/11-25-2014-Boeing-Delivers-Sixth-P-8I-Maritime-Patrol-Aircraft-to-India.*

[42] Sanatu Choudhury, "India Choses Sikorsky for $1 Billion Military Helicopter Deal," *Wall Street Journal*, December 6, 2014. *http://www.wsj.com/articles/india-chooses-sikorsky-for-1-billion-military-helicopter-deal-1417867938.*

[43] "Indian Air Force Chief Says Fighter Jet Deal Soon," *Business World* (India), November 14, 2014. *http://www.businessworld.in/news/economy/indian-air-force-chief-says-fighter-jet-deal-soon/1624031/page-1.html.*

[44] Jay Menon, "Su-30MKI Delivery to Indian Air Force Slips," *Aviation Week*, March 6, 2013. *http://aviationweek.com/defense/su-30mki-delivery-indian-air-force-slips.*

[45] Stockholm International Peace Research Institute, "Transfers of Major Conventional Weapons: Sorted By Supplier. Deals with Deliveries Or Orders Made for Year Range 2004 to 2013," SIPRI Arms Transfer Database, November 10, 2014.

[46] Amrita Dhindsa, "Boeing to Deliver 10 C-17 Airlifters for Indian Air Force by 2014," The Boeing Company, September 15, 2014. *http://www.boeing.co.in/Featured-Content/Boeing-to-build-10-C-17-airlifters-for-Indian-Air.*

[47] Council on Foreign Relations, "China-Pakistan Relations." *http://www.cfr.org/china/china-pakistan-relations/p10070.*

[48] Agence France Presse, "China-Pakistan Friendship 'Sweeter Than Honey', Says Nawaz Sharif," July 5, 2013. *http://www.telegraph.co.uk/news/worldnews/asia/pakistan/10161516/China-Pakistan-friendship-sweeter-than-honey-says-Nawaz-Sharif.html*; *Economist*, "Pakistan and China: Sweet as Can Be? Even an All-Weather Friendship Has its Limits," May 12, 2011. *http://www.economist.com/node/18682839.*

[49] Harsh Pant, "The Pakistan Thorn in China-India-U.S. Relations," *Washington Quarterly* 35:1 (December 2011), p. 84.

[50] Council on Foreign Relations, "China-Pakistan Relations." *http://www.cfr.org/china/china-pakistan-relations/p10070*; Saeed Shah, "Pakistan's Sharif Heading to Beijing to Sign Energy Infrastructure Pacts," *Wall Street Journal*, November 6, 2014. *http://online.wsj.com/articles/pakistans-sharif-heading-to-beijing-to-sign-energy-infrastructure-pacts-1415293363.*

[51] Stockholm International Peace Research Institute, "TIV of Arms Exports to Pakistan, 2004-2013," SIPRI Arms Transfer Database, November 7, 2014. *http://www.sipri.org/databases/armstransfers.*

[52] Stockholm International Peace Research Institute, "Transfers of Major Conventional Weapons: Sorted by Supplier. Deals with Deliveries Or Orders Made for Year Range 2004 To 2013," SIPRI Arms Transfer Database, November 7, 2014.

[53] Forhan Bokhari, "China, Pakistan Set for Submarine Deal by End of Year, Say Officials," *Jane's*, February 2, 2014. *http://www.janes.com/article/33315/china-pakistan-set-for-submarine-deal-by-end-of-year-say-officials.*

[54] The International Institute of Strategic Studies, *The Military Balance 2014* (London, UK: Routledge), p.272.

[55] Ankit Panda, "Pakistan Begins Producing Block-II JF-17 Aircraft," *Diplomat*, December 27, 2013. *http://thediplomat.com/2013/12/pakistan-begins-producing-block-ii-jf-17-aircraft/.*

[56] Council on Foreign Relations, "China-Pakistan Relations." *http://www.cfr.org/china/china-pakistan-relations/p10070.*

[57] John W. Garver, *Protracted Contest: Sino-Indian Rivalry in the Twentieth Century* (Seattle, WA, University of Washington Press, 2001), pp. 327, 329; T.V. Paul, "Chinese-Pakistani Nuclear/Missile Ties and the Balance of Power," *Non-Proliferation Review* (Summer 2003) 4.

[58] T.V. Paul, "Chinese-Pakistani Nuclear/Missile Ties and the Balance of Power," *Non-Proliferation Review* (Summer 2003) 5.

[59] *Hindu*, "We're Fully Alert, Govt on China-Pak Nuke Deal," December 17, 2014. *http://www.thehindu.com/news/national/were-fully-alert-govt-on-chinapak-nuke-deal/article6700916.ece*; Shirley A. Kan, *China and Proliferation of Weapons of Mass Destruction and Missiles: Policy Issues* (Congressional Research Service, November 25, 2014), p. 4.

[60] BBC, "1959: Dalai Lama Escapes to India." *http://news.bbc.co.uk/onthisday/hi/dates/stories/march/31/newsid_2788000/2788343.stm.*

[61] Central Tibetan Administration, "About CTA." *http://tibet.net/about-cta.*

[62] Raja Mohan, *Sino-Indian Rivalry in the Indo-Pacific* (Washington DC: Carnegie Endowment for International Peace, 2012), p. 197.

[63] Ben Blanchard, "Beijing Tells Dalai Lama Again to Respect Reincarnation," Reuters, September 10, 2014. *http://www.reuters.com/article/2014/09/10/us-china-tibet-idUSKBN0H50ST20140910.*

[64] Kieran Cooke, "The Dams of India: Boon or Bane?," *Guardian*, March 17, 2014. *http://www.theguardian.com/environment/2014/mar/17/india-dams-rivers-himalaya-wildlife.*

[65] Agence France-Presse, "China's Mega-Dam in Tibet Begins Operations, India Watches Closely," November 24, 2014. *http://www.ndtv.com/article/india/china-s-mega-dam-in-tibet-begins-operations-india-watches-closely-625096*; *Press Trust of India*, "PM Meets Chinese President, Raises Brahmaputra Issue," March 24, 2013. *http://www.tehelka.com/pm-meets-chinese-president-raises-brahmaputra-issue/.*

[66] Tanvi Madan, "The Modi-Xi Summit and China-India Relations" (Washington, DC: The Brookings Institution, September 16, 2014). *http://www.brookings.edu/research/opinions/2014/09/16-modi-xi-summit-and-china-india-relations?;* Ayeshea Perera, "Live: Must Resolve Boundary Issues with China at the Earliest, Says Modi," *Firstpost* (India), September 18, 2014. *http://www.firstpost.com/world/live-must-resolve-boundary-issues-with-china-at-the-earliest-says-modi-1716009.html;* Ayeshea Perera, "Live: Ladakh Standoff Ends as India and China Retreat," *Firstpost* (India), September 18, 2014.

[67] Data from India's Ministry of Commerce and Industry, via CEIC.

[68] Data from India's Ministry of Commerce and Industry, via CEIC.

[69] Avantika Chilkoti, "India's IT Industry Turns East," *Financial Times*, February 15, 2013. *http://blogs.ft.com/beyond-brics/2013/02/15/indias-it-industry-turns-east/.*

[70] Data from People's Bank of China, via CEIC.

[71] Data from World Bank Development Indicators.

[72] World Economic Forum, *The Global Enabling Trade Report 2014*, (Geneva, Switzerland, 2014) pp. 100, 160. *http://www3.weforum.org/docs/WEF_GlobalEnablingTrade_Report_2014.pdf.*

[73] Data from World Bank Development Indicators.

[74] World Bank Doing Business rankings. *http://www.doingbusiness.org/rankings.*

[75] Data from World Bank Development Indicators.

[76] Karen Eggleston et al., "Will Demographic Change Slow China's Rise?" *Journal of Asian Studies* 72:3 (August 2013) 505.

[77] Worldometers. "Countries in the World (ranked by 2014 population)." *http://www.worldometers.info/world-population/population-by-country.*

[78] Data from World Bank Development Indicators.

[79] M. Taylor Fravel, "China Views India's Rise: Deepening Cooperation, Managing Differences," in Ashley Tellis, Travis Tanner, and Jessica Keogh eds. *Asia Responds to its Rising Powers: China and India* (Seattle, WA, National Bureau of Asian Research, 2011), p. 81.

[80] Andrew North, "Premier Li Keqiang's Visit: India and China in Border Row Pledge," BBC, May 20, 2013. *http://www.bbc.com/news/world-asia-india-22592770.*

[81] Xi Jinping, "Towards an Asian Century of Prosperity," *Hindu*, September 17, 2014. *http://www.thehindu.com/todays-paper/tp-opinion/towards-an-asian-century-of-prosperity/article6417277.ece.*

[82] Ayeshea Perera, "Live: Must Resolve Boundary Issues with China at the Earliest, Says Modi," *First Post* (India), September 18, 2014. *http://www.firstpost.com/world/live-must-resolve-boundary-issues-with-china-at-the-earliest-says-modi-1716009.html.*

[83] Edward Schwarck, "Can China and India Cooperate in Afghanistan?," *Diplomat*, October 1, 2014. *http://thediplomat.com/2014/10/can-china-and-india-cooperate-in-afghanistan/.*

[84] Ministry of External Affairs (India), "Joint Statement between the Republic of India and the People's Republic of China on Building a Closer Developmental Partnership," September 19, 2014. *http://www.mea.gov.in/bilateral-documents.htm?dtl/24022/Joint+Statement+between+the+Republic+of+India+and+the+Peoples+Republic+of+China+on+Building+a+Closer+Developmental+Partnership.*

[85] Jonathan Watts, "China, India Agree to Cooperate on Climate Change Policy," *Guardian*, October 22, 2009. *http://www.theguardian.com/environment/2009/oct/22/china-india-climate-change-cooperation.*

[86] Annie Gowen, "Troops Face off at India-China Border as Nation's Leaders Meet," *Washington Post*, September 18, 2014. *http://www.washingtonpost.com/world/troops-face-off-at-india-china-border-as-leaders-of-nations-meet/2014/09/18/a86e7b8a-1962-4446-b80c-f038a57527f3_story.html.*

[87] Press Trust of India, "China President Xi's India Visit: China Set to Pump Billions of Dollars in India; Outwit Japan," *Economic Times* (India), September 14, 2014. *http://articles.economictimes.indiatimes.com/2014-09-14/news/53904022_1_india-visit-prime-minister-narendra-modi-railway.*

[88] Press Trust of India, "China President Xi's India Visit: China Set to Pump Billions of Dollars in India; Outwit Japan," *Economic Times* (India), September 14, 2014. *http://articles.economictimes.indiatimes.com/2014-09-14/news/53904022_1_india-visit-prime-minister-narendra-modi-railway.*

[89] Embassy of India in China, "Minutes of the First Meeting of the Joint Study Group of the Bangladesh-China-India-Myanmar Economic Corridor (BCIM EC)," December 20, 2013. *http://www.indianembassy.org.cn/newsDetails.aspx?NewsId=455.*

[90] Ministry of External Affairs (India), "Joint Statement between the Republic of India and the People's Republic of China on Building a Closer Developmental Partnership," September 19, 2014. *http://www.mea.gov.in/bilateral-documents.htm?dtl/24022/Joint+Statement+between+the+Republic+of+India+and+the+Peoples+Republic+of+China+on+Building+a+Closer+Developmental+Partnership.*

[91] Bree Feng, "Deal Set on China-Led Infrastructure Bank," *New York Times*, October 24, 2014. *http://www.nytimes.com/2014/10/25/world/asia/china-signs-agreement-with-20-other-nations-to-establish-international-development-bank.html?_r=0.*

[92] *Economic Times* (India), "BASIC Countries Ask Developed Nations to Walk the Talk for Climate Change," August 8, 2014. *http://articles.economictimes.indiatimes.com/2014-08-08/news/52594367_1_environmental-affairs-edna-molewa-durban-platform-climate-change.*

[93] Ankit Panda, "Is Trilateral China-India-Russia Cooperation in Afghanistan Possible?," Diplomat, January 16, 2014. *http://thediplomat.com/2014/01/is-trilateral-china-india-russia-cooperation-in-afghanistan-possible/.*

[94] Li Hong, and Sharon Xiaowen Lin, "Do Emerging Markets Matter in the World Oil Pricing System? Evidence of Imported Crude by China and India," *Energy Policy* 39 (2011): 4624-4630.

[95] Shannon Tiezzi, "In New Plan, China Eyes 2020 Energy Gap," *Diplomat*, November 20, 2014. *http://thediplomat.com/2014/11/in-new-plan-china-eyes-2020-energy-cap/*; Andreas Goldthau, "From the State to the Market and Back: Policy Implications of Changing Energy Paradigms," *Global Policy* 3:2 (May 2012): 205.

[96] R. Evan Ellis, "China, Russia, India, and the Venezuelan Petroleum Industry," *Latin Trade Magazine*, December 11, 2013. *http://latintrade.com/china-russia-india-and-the-venezuelan-petroleum-industry/*; Argus Media, "Caracas Restructures China Oil-Backed Loans," October 28, 2014. *https://www.argusmedia.com/News/Article?id=938771*.

[97] Ben Laidler et al, "South-South Special: What a Globalizing China Means for LatAm" (HSBC Global Research, November 2013), p. 17.

[98] Utpal Bhaskar, "India Trumps China for Brazil Offshore Block," *Mint*, October 15, 2013, via Factiva.

[99] Younkyoo Kim and Fabio Indeo, "The New Great Game in Central Asia Post 2014: The US 'New Silk Road' Strategy and Sino-Russian Rivalry," *Communist and Post-Communist Studies* 46 (2013): 278-283.

[100] "Q4 2013 China Ming Yang Wind Power Group Limited Earnings Conference Call – Final," *CQ FD Disclosure*, April 7, 2014, via Factiva.

[101] Ministry of External Affairs (India), "Joint Statement between the Republic of India and the People's Republic of China on Building a Closer Developmental Partnership," September 19, 2014. *http://www.mea.gov.in/bilateral-documents.htm?dtl/24022/Joint+Statement+between+the+Republic+of+India+and+the+Peoples+Republic+of+China+on+Building+a+Closer+Developmental+Partnership*.

[102] White House, "U.S.-India Joint Statement," September 30, 2014. *http://www.whitehouse.gov/the-press-office/2014/09/30/us-india-joint-statement*; Office of the Spokesperson, U.S. Department of State, "U.S.-India Security Partnership," September 30, 2014. *http://www.state.gov/r/pa/prs/ps/2014/09/232330.htm*.

[103] Agence France-Presse, "India Increases Defense Spending, Invites Foreign Investment," *Defense News*, July 10, 2014. *http://www.defensenews.com/article/20140710/DEFREG03/307100029/India-Increases-Defense-Spending-Invites-Foreign-Investment*.

[104] S. Amer Latif and Nicholas Lombardo, *U.S.-India Defense Trade* (Center for Strategic and International Studies, June 2012), p. 44. *http://csis.org/files/publication/120703_Latif_USIndiaDefense_Web.pdf*.

[105] S. Amer Latif and Nicholas Lombardo, *U.S.-India Defense Trade* (Center for Strategic and International Studies, June 2012), p. 45. *http://csis.org/files/publication/120703_Latif_USIndiaDefense_Web.pdf*.

[106] Stockholm International Peace Research Institute, "TIV of Arms Exports to India, 2004-2013," SIPRI Arms Transfer Database, November 7, 2014. *http://www.sipri.org/databases/armstransfers*.

[107] Stockholm International Peace Research Institute, "TIV of Arms Exports to India, 2004-2013," SIPRI Arms Transfer Database, November 7, 2014. *http://www.sipri.org/databases/armstransfers*.

[108] S. Amer Latif and Nicholas Lombardo, *U.S.-India Defense Trade* (Center for Strategic and International Studies, June 2012), pp. 12-14. *http://csis.org/files/publication/120703_Latif_USIndiaDefense_Web.pdf*; Alan Kronstadt and Sonia Pinto, *U.S.-India Security Relations: Strategic Issues* (Congressional Research Service, January 2013), p. 19.

[109] Sanatu Choudhury, "Defense Deals Likely on Agenda as India's Modi Visits U.S.," *Wall Street Journal*, September 26, 2014. *http://online.wsj.com/articles/defense-deals-likely-on-agenda-as-indias-modi-visits-u-s-1411726479*.

[110] Rama Lakshmi, "India is the World's Largest Arms Importer. It Aims to be a Big Weapon's Dealer, Too," *Washington Post*, November 16, 2014. *http://www.washingtonpost.com/world/asia_pacific/india-is-the-worlds-largest-arms-importer-it-aims-to-be-a-big-weapons-dealer-too/2014/11/15/10839bc9-2627-4a41-a4d6-b376e0f860ea_story.html*.

[111] S. Amer Latif, *U.S.-India Military Engagement: Steady as They Go* (Center for Strategic and International Studies, December 2012), p. 16.

[112] S. Amer Latif, *U.S.-India Military Engagement: Steady as They Go* (Center for Strategic and International Studies, December 2012), pp. 8, 11, 16.

[113] S. Amer Latif, *U.S.-India Military Engagement: Steady as They Go* (Center for Strategic and International Studies, December 2012), p. 22.

[114] S. Amer Latif, *U.S.-India Military Engagement: Steady as They Go* (Center for Strategic and International Studies, December 2012), pp. 34, 39, 40.

[115] *Defence Now,* "India and Singapore Army Hold Annual Joint Military Exercises." *http://www.defencenow.com/news/103/india-and-singapore-army-hold-annual-joint-military-exercises.html*.

[116] Niharika Mandhana, "Japan to Join U.S.-India Military Exercises," *Wall Street Journal*, July 22, 2014. *http://online.wsj.com/articles/japan-to-join-u-s-india-military-exercises-1406043468*.

[117] *Shifting Composition of Asian-Pacific Security Architecture* (Asia Pacific Foundation of Canada, February 2014), *http://www.asiapacific.ca/sites/default/files/security_architecture_v4.pdf*.

[118] Sanjeev Miglani, "India to Supply Vietnam with Naval Vessels amid China Disputes," Reuters, October 28, 2014. *http://in.reuters.com/article/2014/10/28/india-vietnam-idINKBN0IH0L020141028*; Sudhi Ranjan Sen, "To Counter China, Indian BrahMos Missiles, Patrol Boats for Vietnam?," *NDTV* (India), October 28, 2014. *http://www.ndtv.com/article/india/to-counter-china-indian-brahmos-missiles-patrol-boats-for-vietnam-612652*.

[119] Vivek Raghuvanshi, "Indo-S. Korean Defense Ties Deepen with Minesweeper Purchase," *Defense News*, October 15, 2013.*http://www.defensenews.com/article/20131015/DEFREG03/310150015/Indo-S-Korean-Defense-Ties-Deepen-Minesweeper-Purchase*.

[120] Ministry of External Affairs (India), *Tokyo Declaration for India - Japan Special Strategic and Global Partnership*, September 1, 2014.

*http://www.mea.gov.in/bilateral-documents.htm?dtl/23965/Tokyo+Declaration+for+India++Japan+Special+Strategic+and+Global+Partnership.*

[121] U.S. Pacific Command, *PACOM Senate Armed Services Committee Posture Statement,* March 25, 2014. *http://www.pacom.mil/Media/SpeechesTestimony/tabid/6706/Article/8598/pacom-senate-armed-services-committee-posture-statement.aspx.*

[122] Patrick M. Cronin et al., *The Emerging Asia Power Web: The Rise of Bilateral Intra-Asian Security Ties* (Center for a New S. American Security, June 2013), p. 24.

[123] Rory Medcalf, *Responding to Indo-Pacific Rivalry: Australia, India, and Middle Power Coalitions* (Lowy Institute for International Policy, August 8, 2014), p. 14.

[124] Patrick M. Cronin et al., *The Emerging Asia Power Web: The Rise of Bilateral Intra-Asian Security Ties* (Center for a New S. American Security, June 2013), p. 32.